D1256465

THE INTERNET LIBRARY

Creating Animation for Your Web Page

Gerry, Janet, and Allison Souter

Enslow Publishers, Inc.

40 Industrial Road   PO Box 38
Box 398   Aldershot
Berkeley Heights, NJ 07922   Hants GU12 6BP
USA   UK

http://www.enslow.com

Copyright © 2003 by Enslow Publishers, Inc.

All rights reserved.

No part of this book may be reproduced by any means
without the written permission of the publisher.

Library of Congress Cataloging-in-Publication Data

Souter, Gerry.
   Creating animation for your Web page / Gerry, Janet & Allison Souter.
      p. cm. — (The Internet library)
Contents: Types of animation — GIF animations — Animating with GIF
Construction Set — Animating with GifBuilder — Java Applets —
JavaScript — Flash and QuickTime.
   ISBN 0-7660-2083-5
   1. Computer animation—Juvenile literature. 2. Web sites—Design—
Juvenile literature. [1. Computer animation. 2. Web sites—Design.]
I. Souter, Janet, 1940-   II. Souter, Allison.
III. Title. IV. Series.
TR897.7.S68 2003
006.6'96—dc21
                              2002152960

Printed in the United States of America

10 9 8 7 6 5 4 3 2 1

To Our Readers:
We have done our best to make sure all Internet addresses in this book were
active and appropriate when we went to press. However, the author and the
publisher have no control over and assume no liability for the material
available on those Internet sites or on other Web sites they may link to. Any
comments or suggestions can be sent by e-mail to comments@enslow.com
or to the address on the back cover.

Trademarks:
Most computer and software brand names have trademarks or registered
trademarks. The individual trademarks have not been listed here.

Cover Photo: Photo illustration by Sana Fazai

Contents

Introduction

This is my friend Web. He will be appearing throughout the pages of this book to guide you through the information presented here and to take you to a variety of Internet sites and activities. Web is also a reminder that there is always more to learn about the Internet.

When you log on to Web sites while doing research, you probably spend more time browsing the sites that have what we might call "pizzazz." These sites use words and pictures that are moving, spinning, blinking, and scrolling. All that action comes from Web animation.

Maybe animation began when prehistoric man first drew a picture of an animal and decided he wanted to show it running. He did so by drawing lots of legs to show the different positions they would be in as the animal ran.

Most animation is a series of still pictures viewed in a fast-moving sequence to look like action. You've seen flip books with images that change slightly with each page. As the pages are flipped, the picture appears to be moving, such as a girl dancing or a dog running. The invention of the motion picture camera showed animation to larger audiences. The first attempts used the same principle that's used in the flip books. They were black-and-white still pictures photographed one frame at a time. Each frame showed for only a fraction of a second. When the film was projected on the screen, it looked as though the drawings were moving. Those Saturday morning cartoons you watch are animated films.

Like a flip book or a cartoon, an animation on the Web can be a series of drawings shown quickly one right after the other, like a movie. It can also be text scrolling across the screen with a message. Animation can be a word blinking on and off, or a button that moves when you click on it. It can even be used in a game. The animation can play automatically and keep running forever, or you can control how long it runs. Animation on the Web can even be controlled by the user.

There's a wide range of possibilities. But an animation created for the Web is usually much smaller and simpler than Saturday morning cartoons. It needs to download quickly onto the page so the viewer won't get bored and leave the site.

Why do people put animations on Web pages? Mostly to attract attention. When you open a page on the Web, your eye is attracted to the blinking banners, scrolling text, or moving pictures. But too much movement can be annoying. One or two active images are usually enough.

Hi! I'm Web.
I'll be giving you useful tips and pointers along the way.

What tool you use depends on what you want to animate and why. Maybe you just want to spice up the page. Imagine you're into astronomy and you want a banner of sparkling stars and a planet or two. You'll probably want to use something called an animated GIF file. In the following chapters, we'll show you what an animated GIF is and how to make one.

If you want a message to scroll across your page, we'll show you how to download and modify a Java applet. No, this is not a small apple from an island in Indonesia. Java is a computer language. We'll show what Java and applets can do for your Web site in chapter 3. We'll also talk about JavaScript (completely different from Java applets, despite the similar name). These "scripts" let users control the animations on your page.

Once you're comfortable with all the animation tools out there, you can have a lot of fun. Some browsers don't support the special tools you need to show an animation on your site. We'll show you which browsers work with which type of animations so you can create one that most visitors to your Web page can see.

Chapter 1

Types of Animation

Why add an animation to your Web site? There are plenty of reasons. You might want to draw attention to something you've added to your page. Let's say your site is about model airplanes. To jazz it up a bit, you might want to show a jet zooming across the top of your home page. When you need to show how something works, there's nothing like an animation. For instance, you can show how a seed becomes a plant for your science class, or how the planets rotate around the sun.

Once you've decided to add animation, you can create it yourself or download a free animation from other Web sites. There are lots of sites available that offer different types of animations, from simple animated GIF files to complex Java applets. (We'll discuss those in the upcoming chapters.)

This chapter will show you different types of animation and give you an idea of how the animation illusion is created and what's involved with each step.

When creating your own animations, it's important to remember a couple of things:

- *Keep the file size small.* The general rule when designing Web pages for a large audience is to keep the entire page, including artwork and

HTML, under 60 k. When planning your animation, take into account the size of all the other files that are part of the page and plan accordingly.

- *Keep your ideas simple.* You're just starting out. There's plenty of time for you to learn to do more complicated things later on.

▶ Setting Up a Practice Page

Before we get started, let's create a page that lets us test our animations and make sure they work before uploading them to the Web.

Open up a word processing program on your computer and type the following:

```
<html>
```

```
<head>
```

```
<title>My Animation Web
Site</title>
```
(Text that goes in the title bar of the window)

```
</head>
```

```
<body bgcolor="#FFFFFF">
```
(Makes the background white)

```
<div align="center">
```
(Aligns the heading in the center top part of the page)

```
<h1>
```
(Text will be formatted to Heading 1 style)

Parts List:

Keep a list of the sizes of all the elements on your page, such as text, photos, drawings, and sound clips, as you assemble it. That way, you'll know how much room to allow for your animation.

Animation Art List:

```
<b><font color="#0000CC">My Anima-
tion Web Site</font></b>
```
(The text that appears on the page will be "My Animation Web Site" and it will be blue [0000CC])

```
</h1>
```

```
</div>
```

You've now created a Web page with a white background and blue text at the top that reads "My Animation Web Site." Save this file as an htm document (you can name it Animation.htm) and let's get started!

▶ Two-Step Animation

The simplest animation is a two-step animation, which consists of two images or frames. If you show these two images in sequence over and over again, it looks like the words What's New! are blinking on and off. This is called looping.

Frame 1   Frame 2

▶ Motion Animation

Simple motion animation consists of one drawing that you "slide" from one edge of the frame to the other.

Frame 1

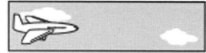

Frame 2

Frame 3

Frame 4

Frame 5

Frame 6

Frame 7

The background can be plain or, like this one, it can contain a few simple shapes. We wanted the plane to look as though it was zooming across the sky. We took one drawing of the plane, put it at the far left of the screen, and saved that as frame 1. Then we moved the plane over a little and saved that as frame 2, and so on until we got to frame 7.

This is a simple animation because the plane has no moving parts. The more frames you use to move it across the sky, the smoother the animation will be. However, the more frames you use, the bigger the file size, which means it will take longer to load onto your page. You'll need to experiment to see how many frames you'll need to get the effect you want but keep the file size small. Again, the more complex the drawing, the bigger the file size.

▶ Cycle Animation

Two-step animation is actually cycle animation, but now we'll talk about animations that need more than two frames to work. Suppose you want to make a wheel rotate. You need more than two images. You need three.

If you play these three frames over and over (called looping, remember?), it will look as though the wheel is spinning. The trick is to make sure the number of spokes you have can be divided evenly into three. This wheel has twelve spokes. You could also make this work using only three spokes, or six or nine or fifteen and so on.

Keep It Simple:
When starting out, try to use simple backgrounds and limit the animation to small, eye-catching surprises.

See how the black spoke starts at the top? In the next frame, we moved all the black spokes over one. We did the same with the gray and the white. In the third frame, we moved each of them over one again.

 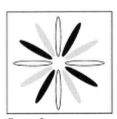 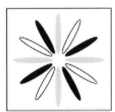

Frame 1   Frame 2   Frame 3

This effect also works in creating a "marquee." You've seen marquees on the neon signs over theater entrances. Usually, there are colored lights that seem to be moving around the edge of the sign. We're just building a smaller version.

When this animation is looped, it will look as though the black dots are travelling around the square. Once again, we made sure that the number of dots can be divided evenly by three. There are 12 dots.

These types of animation are simple because they require only three frames to work, and the drawings are easy to create. You can control the speed of the animation by changing the amount of time each frame is on the screen.

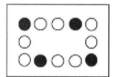
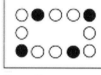
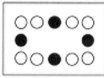

Frame 1   Frame 2   Frame 3

Another kind of cycle animation is a person walking or a butterfly flapping its wings. It usually takes more than three frames to cover the whole sequence of movement. Once you draw them, you can loop them over and over. You can keep the animated drawings in one place, like the butterfly below. You can also shift each frame as you draw it so that the butterfly looks as though it's fluttering around the screen.

This animation is more complex because it consists of four different frames. You see six, you say? But the key word here is *different*. Frames 1 through 4 are the first half of the sequence. When

Frame 1   Frame 2   Frame 3   Frame 4   Frame 5   Frame 6

the butterfly's wings are closed, they need to open again. Rather than draw another frame, we simply copied frame 3 and named it frame 5. Frame 6 is the same drawing as frame 2, so you really only have to create four drawings.

This type of animation also uses something called key frames. In creating this butterfly, we drew frame 1 first. That is the key frame. We knew that the picture of the wings fully closed would be the end of the first half of the sequence, or frame 4. Frame 4 is a key frame because it is the halfway point of the sequence. The wings are closed all the way before they start to open again.

Key frames are like guideposts for the movement you want to create. Once they are in place, you can fill in the frames that go in between so the movement appears smooth. This is called in-betweening or tweening. Frames 2, 3, 5, and 6 are the in-between frames of this animation.

Another thing to decide is how long each frame should appear on the screen. If you have each frame on the screen for the same amount of time (say, 1 second), the butterfly's motion will be too regular and won't look natural. When we animated this butterfly, we kept frame 1 up for the longest amount of time, then frame 2, a little less; frame 3, even less than that; and frame 4, for half the time as frame 1. But then we made frame 5 a little longer and frame 6, longer still. When the animation plays, it looks fairly natural.

Choppy Can Be Cool:
How fast an animation plays can vary from one browser to another. Movement that is choppy will play on all browsers. Design your timing so that choppy is cool, and no matter the browser, your animation will rule.

Another thing to consider is that this butterfly stays in one place. If you want it to flutter around a flower, it will take more time and be a bigger file size because you will have to repeat the sequence of six frames as you move the butterfly around the flower's petals.

The great thing about making an animation, though, is that things don't have to move naturally if you don't want them to. We can give feet to that butterfly and have it do a dance. We can zoom it across the screen like an airplane. We can also exaggerate movement to make it easier to see. This is called squash and stretch. A simple example of this is in the illustration of the bouncing ball. When the ball hits the floor, we squash the shape to make the impact look really big. The stretch happens an instant later, when our shape bounces on the way to getting back to its original shape.

▶ Frame-by-Frame Non-Looping Animation

This kind of animation is generally something you don't loop. The artwork changes in every frame, such as in the case of a seed growing into a plant. This type of animation can get very complex. It can take a lot of frames, depending on what you are trying to show.

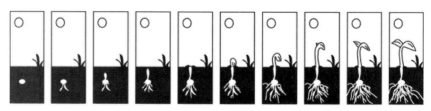

Frame 1   Frame 2   Frame 3   Frame 4   Frame 5   Frame 6   Frame 7   Frame 8   Frame 9   Frame 10

Keep in mind that if your animation file gets too big, your visitors will have to sit there yawning while it loads. Don't overdo it!

This chapter has introduced you to some of the most basic concepts of animation. Using these techniques, you can control time by breaking down a movement into pieces. Then you can reassemble it with an illusion of motion. You can control the direction of movement and how long it takes to play. It's a lot of fun to fool the eye.

Now that you've seen some examples of simple animation, you'll think of others. You can have fun experimenting with the possibilities. Let's see how creative you can be.

Chapter 2

GIF Animations

You may remember that we talked about animated GIFs in the introduction. The letters stand for *graphic interchange format*. GIFs are graphics file formats that are commonly used in Web pages for several reasons.

- They compress to a small file size.
- They are accepted by all types of browsers.
- They require no special plug-in (special attached software program) to view.
- You can insert them onto your Web page the same way you insert an image, using the "img src" element.
- They can be still images or animated images.
- They can have transparent backgrounds.
- They can be created with a simple paint program.
- Animated GIFs can be assembled with inexpensive (or even free) authoring tools available for download from the Internet.

Sounds cool, right? In HTML, there's no difference between adding an animated GIF and a still-image GIF to your Web site. The code is the same because the GIF allows for many images to be contained in one file. GIFs can have transparent backgrounds, so you can have an animation play over a background that has a pattern without having the animation surrounded by a box. It's a wonderful file format for small looping cartoons, rotating logos, animated button rollovers, or any type of simple, drawn animation.

GIF files have some limitations. They can contain no more than 256 colors. Because they are compressed to keep them small, it's best to use the GIF file format for drawings and plain text. You can't make GIF animations interactive. They simply load onto the page and play according to the way they were constructed (playing only once, looping a certain number of times, or looping continuously). They can't contain audio. Nevertheless, you can have fun with GIFs, and they are a good learning tool for creating Web animation.

▶ Finding Animated GIFs on the Web

Before you try creating your own GIF images to animate your Web site, take a look at some of the free ones that are available. There are waving hands, rotating globes (with clouds), spinning soccer balls, moving cars, and much more. Two good free sites are

http://www.eclipsed.com

http://www.gifanimations.com

There are lots of others. If you type "GIF animation free" in Google Search, you'll get a nice, long list of choices. Keep in mind that some sites ask that you link the images back to their Web site or that you mention where you got them. Others may look as if they're free but really just "tease" you to buy something—or the free images aren't that great anyway. In some cases, you may suddenly find yourself at a Web page that is definitely not meant for kids. So, read carefully and check with your parents or a teacher if you aren't sure.

Have you already found a GIF you'd like to put on your Web site? At the end of chapter 3, you'll learn how to do that, so feel free to skip to page 35.

▶ Creating Your Own Animated GIFs

Animated GIFs are made up of a series of still images that are also called GIFs. The first step in making an animated GIF is creating the images you want to animate. There are a number of inexpensive paint programs you can use to do this. Some can be downloaded from the Web. To find paint software that is free, try

http://www.kidsfreeware.com

Most PCs and Macs come with paint programs built into their operating systems that let you save images in a GIF format. Also, Paint Shop Pro comes with an animation program to make animated GIFs.

Here are a couple of things to remember when building and saving the images you are going to animate.

First, when you save the files, number them in the order they are going to appear in the animation. If you are going to animate a bird flying, you might name the files Bird01.gif, Bird02.gif, Bird03.gif, and so on.

Second, try to keep the file sizes of your animation as small as possible. You'll need to experiment to get the nicest animation possible at the smallest size. You want it to look great, but you don't want people waiting for a long time to see it. If you're adding animation to your page to spice it up, then your file sizes should stay between 7 and 15 kilobytes. You'll be able to accomplish a lot, and you can keep the files small simply by drawing them small and limiting the number of colors you use.

When all your drawings are complete and saved, you are ready to assemble them in an animation. There are programs available on the Web that assemble individual GIF drawings into an animation. You can download them and install them on your computer, and they are available for both Windows and Mac operating systems. Two of the most popular are GIF Construction Set for Windows and GifBuilder for the Mac. The Web sites at which you can find these programs are listed on page 21. But before you go there, you should get permission from from your parents or another responsible adult.

GifBuilder, created by Yves Piguet, is used for the Mac, and the good news is, it's free. You can download it from any number of shareware or freeware sites. There are a few listed below. Instructions on how to install GifBuilder are included and easy to follow. Please ask an adult to help you out with this.

GIF Audio Tip:
A GIF animation can't contain audio, but there's no reason you can't create a separate audio file that loads and plays at the same time. Early silent movies had a piano player or band in the theater to play along with the action.

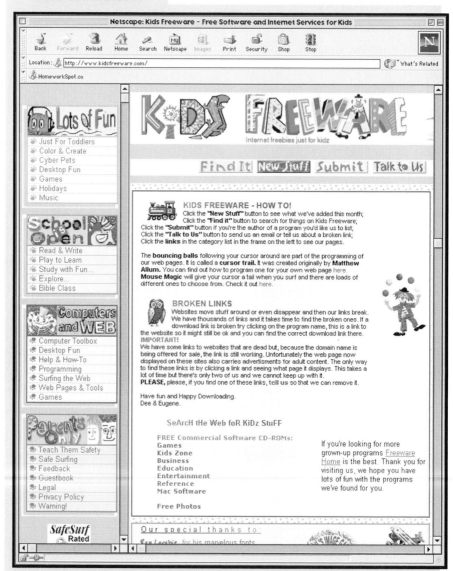

There are lots of sites on the Web where free GIF animations and short programs can be downloaded. Be sure to give the site credit for what you've borrowed.

http://homepage.mac.com/piguet/gif.html

http://www.download.com

http://www.shareware.com

The Windows program, GIF Construction Set Professional, costs around $20. But you can try it out for a while for free. You can download it from

http://www.mindworkshop.com/
alchemy/gifcon.html

It also comes with instructions for installing it on your system.

The next two chapters will show you quick, step-by-step ways to create animated GIFs in each of these programs. Most GIF animation programs are created in more or less the same way. If you are using some other program, this will still give you an idea of how animated GIFs are put together and what to look for. Following these tutorials is information about some of the ways you can make changes to your GIF file. Chapter 3 shows you how to put an animated GIF onto your Web page.

Using Zeroes:
Include a zero in front of single numbers when naming files: 01, 02, 03, etc. That way, if you have more than 10 files, they will appear in order when you load them. If you don't, it might look like this: bird1.gif, bird11.gif, bird12.gif...

Animating With GIF Construction Set

Below is a list of terms associated with animated GIF files. They will help you to understand the choices you are given when creating your animations. Different programs may refer to them in different ways, but the general ideas are the same.

Background Color: If you want a transparent GIF, keep your drawing on a solid background color that is similar to the background on which the GIF image will play. You can then set that color to be transparent.

Colors and Depth (Palettes): Most GIF programs allow you to optimize the color palette so you can make the file as small as possible. They usually offer a number of choices on how to handle the color palette, depending on whether your image is a simple drawing or a complex photograph. Experiment with the different settings and see how they affect how the image looks as well as the file size.

Delay: In most GIF animation programs, 100 equals 1 second; 50 equals half a second; 1200 equals 12 seconds. You can have all the frames of your animation appear for the same amount of time, or you can go into each individual frame and have it up on the screen for its own specific time. Don't use 0; some Web browsers may not recognize it.

Disposal Method/Remove By: You have to deal with this option only if your animated GIF has a transparent background. If it has a solid background, then you can usually keep the settings on default (usually called "Nothing"). If your animation is transparent, choose the option that hides the previous frame before the next one pops up. For example, say you have an animation of a person walking across the screen over a transparent background. If you don't hide the previous image, then every frame of the animation will stay up there and be seen through the transparent background, leaving a trail of people across the screen. Experiment with the different settings of this option. Beware that some are not compatible with all browsers.

Dithering: This puts tiny dots of color in your images, like little dabs of paint. It can make your colors and images look better but can make your file size larger. If you use it, just make sure the file doesn't get too large.

Image Size Width: Measurement of the image in pixels.

Interlace: This option lets your GIF file load big chunks of the image a little at a time so that the person viewing your Web site can get an

In a Dither:
If you look up dither in the dictionary, you'll see it means to be nervous or agitated. In computer-speak, to dither a graphic means to fill in the gaps and smooth it out. If you do too much dithering with your animation, you'll be nervous and agitated when you see how much your file has grown!

idea of what's coming rather than looking at a blank space until the entire GIF is loaded. Some people think this saves time, but others find it annoying. This option isn't used very often.

Looping: This option programs your animation to play over and over again.

Transparent Color/Background: Use this option if you want a part of your image transparent so that it plays over an existing patterned background. (You'll need to set the "Disposal Method/Remove By" value. See definition on previous page.)

Okay, you have your GIF animation program. Let's say you want to tell people about your favorite movies. You might want the first page to show an image resembling a movie marquee. How about making a rectangular shape with blinking lights around the edges, with the words "My Favorite Movies" inside it? You'd need to draw three slightly different images. The colors of the "lights" should shift with each drawing. Remember, the number of "lights" must be divisible by three. (You may want to refer back to chapter 1, in which we discuss wheel and marquee animation.)

Number your images according to the order in which they appear. We have named ours movie01.gif, movie02.gif, and movie 03.gif. Also, keep them the same pixel size, and store all your images in the same folder.

These are the GIF files we'll use to make the animation. GIF Construction Set will later compress these into one file.

movie01.gif

movie02.gif

movie03.gif

STEP 1:

Open the GIF Construction Set program by double-clicking this icon.

STEP 2:

The easiest way to get started is to use what's called the Wizard. Click on the magic wand icon, and the program will walk you through the assembling of your images into an animation file.

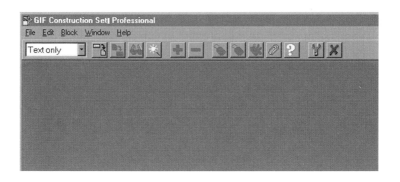

STEP 3:

Click on Next to begin.

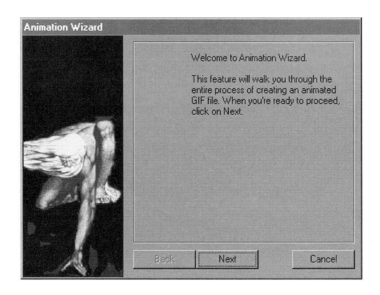

STEP 4:

You are creating this to put on your Web page, so choose the top option.

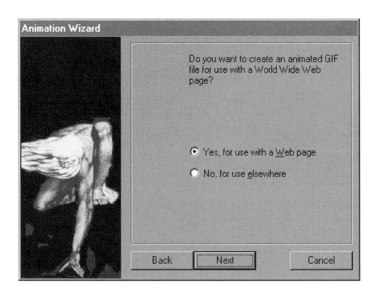

STEP 5:

Since this is a marquee, you'll want it to keep looping over and over again. Choose "Loop indefinitely." Once you've built the animation, you might want to go back and change this to loop only a certain number of times.

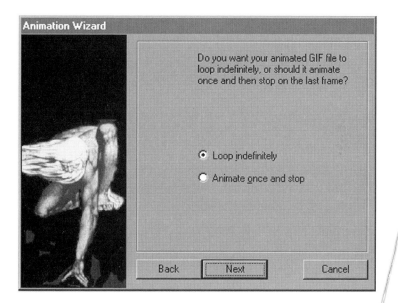

STEP 6:

This screen is asking you to decide on the color palette for your GIF file, so let's go through them one by one.

Matched to super palette means that the Wizard checks the colors in your animation's images and uses a 256-color palette that works best for all your images. It then fixes all the colors in your images to this palette. This gives you the best results.

Dithered to super palette puts tiny dots of color in your images, giving more color variety within your images. This may work better for photos but isn't always necessary for drawings. This is not the right choice for our marquee animation, which is a simple animation.

Matched to first palette builds your animation using the palette of the first image in your animation. You may notice wild color changes in some of the following images if the colors are very different from the first, so be careful. Again, since this is a fairly simple animation, that may not be a problem.

Photorealistic dithers (puts dots in) your images and gives you a palette for building an animation from a true-color image, such as an actual digital photo file, which could have a great many colors. Since GIF is limited in its color offerings, the final result may look grainy. Photorealistic decides on the best palette for the Web.

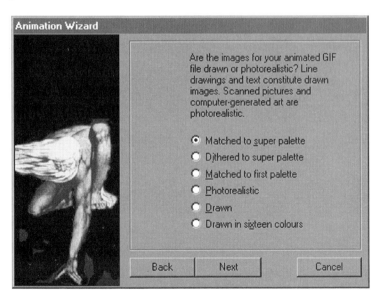

Drawn gives you the same palette as Photorealistic but doesn't dither.

Drawn in sixteen colors is similar to the Drawn option but, as it says, it gives you only the basic Windows 16-color palette.

Experiment with these settings and see what they do to your drawings to understand how they work. Also, look at the file size of your GIF and see how these settings can affect that. For your purposes, select "Matched to super palette."

STEP 7:

Timing is important. If you want the lights to blink or an image to move quickly, choose a smaller number. Since you're creating a marquee effect, you want those lights to blink rapidly. Ten hundredths is a good choice to start. The 100 hundredths choice equals one second. When you begin to animate, you will discover that one second can

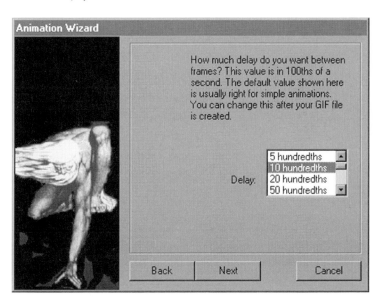

seem like a very long time. You can go back and change the timing for individual frames once everything is assembled.

STEP 8:

Look in the directory where your images are stored. You can select all of them by holding down the Shift key as you click on each file. Click Open when all the files are selected. The Wizard will automatically take you back to this dialogue box to select more images. When you're through, just click Cancel, and it will take you to the next step.

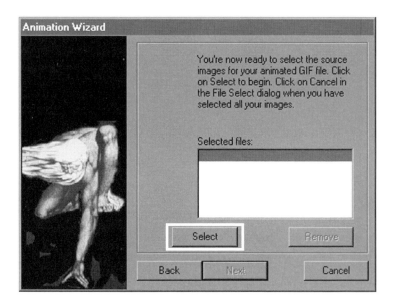

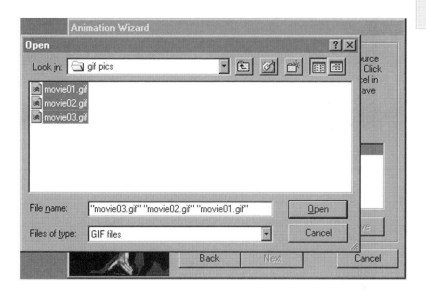

STEP 9:

This one's easy. Click on Done.

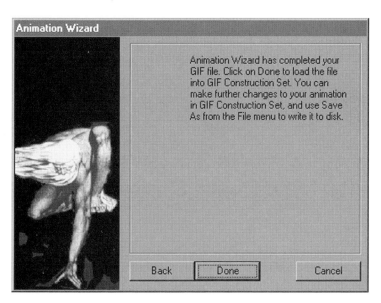

STEP 10:

You can see that the three images of your animation are loaded in sequence.

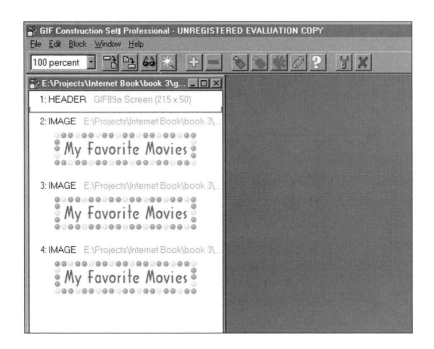

STEP 11:

By double-clicking on an image (as you can see here, we've clicked on the top one), you get a dialogue box that allows you to change the length of time that image stays on the screen and lets you choose whether you want the background to be transparent.

If you want to play around with GIF Construction Set but don't have time to create the drawings for your animation, you can load a completed animation and experiment with that.

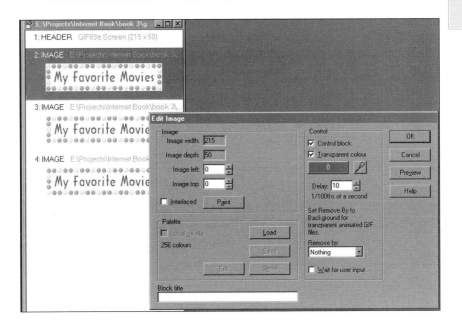

STEP 12:

Double-clicking on Header gives you access to a dialogue box that allows you to make changes for the whole animation. For example, you can choose

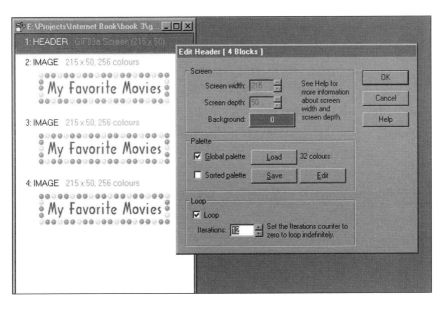

whether you want to loop it over and over or only a certain number of times.

STEP 13:

When you click on the sunglasses icon, you can view your animation and see if it is moving as fast or slow as you want, if it is looping properly, and so on. If everything turns out exactly the way you want, then save it. Let's save this file as movieanim.gif.

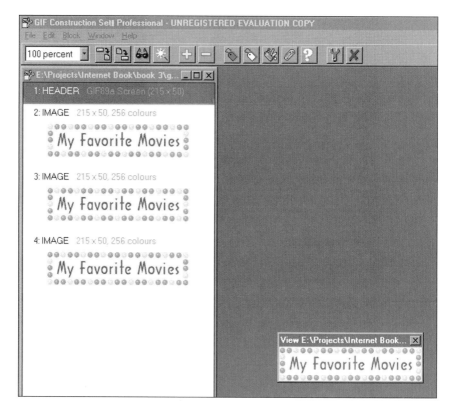

GIF Construction Set gives the PC owner complete creative control of the animation process. Just follow the menus and, with a little practice, some really fun animations are possible.

▶ Putting Your Animation On Your Web Page

Now it's time to put your creation on a Web page. What's great about GIF animations is that the Internet treats them the same way it treats images, so the code is the same. Open up the HTML file we created in chapter 1. We want this animation to sit at the top of the page and be centered, so, after the body bgcolor line, add

```
<div align="center">
```

Then, type in your image.

```
<img src="movieanim.gif"
width="215" height="50">
```

If you've put the GIF animation in a separate images folder with all the other artwork for your site, the code should look like this:

```
<img src="images/movieanim.gif"
width="215" height="50">
```

The final lines of code look like this:

```
<html>

<head>

<title>My Animation Web Site</title>

</head>

 <body bgcolor="#FFFFFF">

  <div align="center">
```

```
<img src="images/movieanim.gif"
width="215" height="50">

</div>

</body>

</html>
```

If you've spent some time experimenting with animation programs, you can see there are lots of ways to have fun adding action to your Web site. As you become more comfortable with animation programs, you may want to check out Web sites that help you create even more exciting Web pages. For example, try

http://www.lissaexplains.com/intro.shtml

It's a site just for kids with a lot of information about HTML.

Good luck and have fun!

Chapter 4

Animating With GifBuilder

f you have a Mac, you can use the GifBuilder program. With GifBuilder, you can open an existing animated GIF to edit or create your own animated GIF. GifBuilder also allows you to open other graphic file formats.

Now we'll show you step-by-step how to create the "My Favorite Movies" animation using GifBuilder on your Mac.

After you've downloaded and installed GifBuilder onto your machine, follow these instructions.

STEP 1:

Open the GifBuilder program by double-clicking this icon.

GifBuilder

STEP 2:

You'll see two windows pop up. Next, open the folder in which you've saved all your GIF drawings.

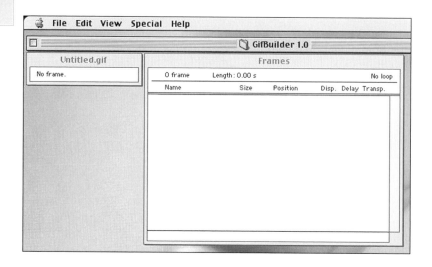

STEP 3:

Drag those files into the Frames window. You now have an animated GIF. It's that simple. Click on the Frames box and the menu bar for GifBuilder to appear. You can go up to Animation and click on Start. Your animation will play once and stop. With

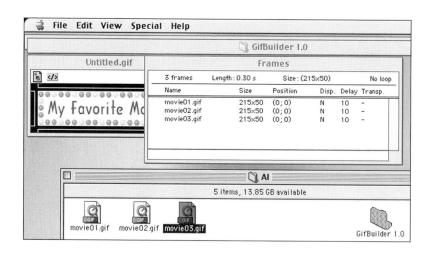

this marquee, you want it to loop a few times. Before you change that, we'll save this file as movieanim.gif. It's always a good idea to save files as you work.

LOOPING YOUR ANIMATED GIF

Here's how to make an animation loop. Click on Options on the menu bar, and select Loop.

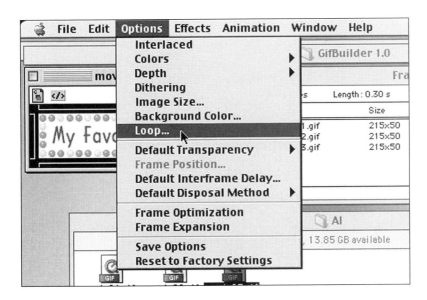

A box pops up giving you the option of not looping, looping forever, or looping a certain number of times. For now, let's have your animation continue looping as long as the page is open—in other words, forever.

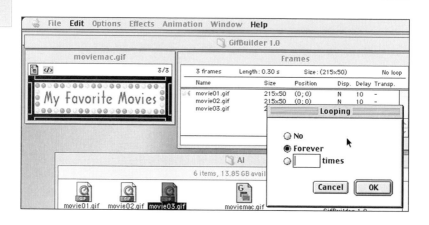

VIEWING YOUR ANIMATION

To view the animation, go to Animation and click Start. If it looks good to you, save the file again and you're finished.

GifBuilder also allows you to do other things with your animation.

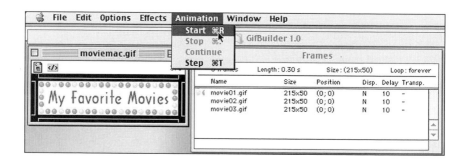

OTHER OPTIONS

You can make the background transparent.

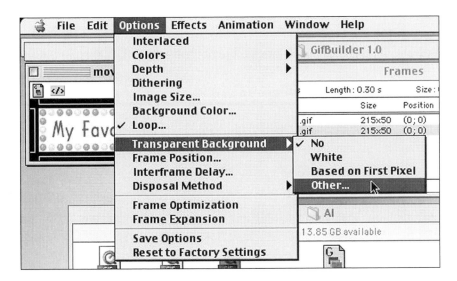

You can make the file smaller by optimizing the color palette.

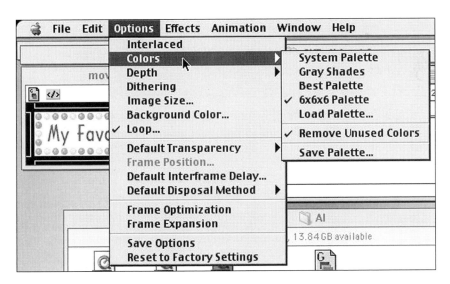

Now that you have your animation all set up and ready to go, turn back to page 35 to learn how to put your animated GIF on your Web page. Good luck!

Java Applets

If you've been exploring the Internet for a while, you've probably come across something called Java. You might have heard someone say, "That game on the Web was done in Java." Well, you're pretty sure they're not talking about either an island in Indonesia or a type of coffee, and you're right. They're talking about a programming language.

▶ What Are They?

If you've ever gone to a Web site and played a little game or seen a great visual effect on a photo (like shimmering water), a three-dimensional cube that rotates when you roll your mouse over it, or text that scrolls across the screen, there's a good chance you've seen a Java applet in action.

Java is a full computer programming language released in 1995 by Sun Microsystems. It was created to run on PC, Mac, or network computers. Its programs can run alongside other computer operating systems. There are many books in the library and a lot of information online about Java programming.

Maybe you're wondering how much work it's going to take to learn this programming language so you can use it. Well, don't worry. The Java that concerns us comes in preprogrammed bits called applets. Programmers write these applets, and some post them on Web sites for others to download and use. As a matter of courtesy, you should give credit to the creator of the applet you use.

It's these applets that create scrolling text, blinking signs, and other special effects. When you use an applet, you don't generally see the code that's making it work. That code is kept in a CLASS file.

The browser calls the applet when an <Applet/> tag is recognized in the HTML code, much like it calls for a picture with an <IMG SRC=> tag. When the browser sees an applet tag, it executes the correct CLASS file. Java applets sit "outside" the HTML code, like a picture or an animation. They are downloaded the same way, so, if it's a big applet, the user might have to wait awhile before seeing it. However, unlike a GIF animation, you have to make sure that the people who are visiting your site have browsers that know what to do with a Java applet. Visitors who have older browsers will see only a line of text that tells them they can't see the Java applet.

Picking Applets:
When you find an applet you like, copy it to a file folder for later use. This way, you can build a library of applets. Then you can use an applet any time you want without having to hunt for the right one.

▶ Adding a Java Applet to Your Web Page

Why use a Java applet to add an animation to your page? Why not just create an animated GIF? Maybe you want to add an interesting effect to a photo or you want text to scroll across the screen. You might be able to do this with a GIF, but it would take a lot of extra work.

Java animations are different from GIF animations in that they are not made up of frame-by-frame pictures. The effects are generated through the programming code. This means that if you have a picture of a lake you want on your Web site, you can download an applet that makes a rippling-water effect and insert the name of the photograph image file in the appropriate place. When you view that photo in a browser, it is rippling! That's much easier and less time-consuming than trying to draw the ripples frame by frame.

Java applet animations also let you do fun things with text. You can move words across the screen in a wavy line like a snake, have them fade in and out, change color, and even get eaten by munching teeth. You can change your text as often as you want by just typing new words into the text portion of your HTML code. It takes only a few minutes, so you can keep up-to-date information, like special announcements, on your Web site.

If you want to see some examples of animating text or a graphic on your page, the place to go is a Web site that has Java applets you can use for free. Before you do this, it's always a good idea to ask a supervising adult for permission first—especially if you're building a Web page on a school computer. Visit the sites and look through the special effects options together.

Two sites that offer free applets to download are

http://www.javaboutique.com
http://www.java.sun.com

We'll walk you through the steps of downloading an applet from one of those sites. There are lots of different sites, but this experience should introduce you to some of the issues you'll face when you visit them.

Suppose you have an announcement you want to post on your Web site about selling candy to raise money for your band to buy new instruments. An announcement in an animated banner running across the top of your home page would certainly attract attention.

The first step is to find a banner applet that you like. We went to www.javaboutique.com to see what was available in special effects text scrollers. You can follow along if you're reading this book in front of a computer logged onto the Internet.

Web sites that provide free Java applets are usually crammed full of useful information and can be a little overwhelming at first. The best thing to do is look for a link called "Applets," "Free Applets," or something similar. We found applets in a column on the left side of JavaBoutique's home page. Under it was a list of pages that sorted applets by category, date, name, Hall of Fame, and so on.

Your first stop is Applets by Category. This page will give you a good idea of all the many different things you can do with Java applets. You need a text effect, and you're in luck, because Text Effects is one of the categories. Scroll through, and, when you click on one, JavaBoutique displays a sample of what that applet does and tells you how to download it and put it on your Web page. There are some pretty cool effects available but unfortunately none that seem to say "Buy some awesome candy!"

In the Hall of Fame category, there's an applet that we liked called ChompText. Click on it and go to the page that tells you all about the applet and shows a sample of a little Pacman-like animation moving across the screen, eating all the text in its path. Perfect.

Most Java applets you download come in a compressed file format. This compressed file can contain the Java applet (a CLASS file), an image file, or animation (in this case, the chomping animation), and anything else you need to copy it onto your system to make it run. You uncompress the file once it's downloaded by using a compression/decompression utility. For ChompText, JavaBoutique provides a link to a Web site from which you can download an uncompressing utility.

ChompText: Won't your visitors be amused when the Chomper starts eating up your text!

On the ChompText page, there's also a sample HTML source. That's the code you're going to copy and paste into your HTML file. After downloading the compressed Pacman animation file, go back to the JavaBoutique Web page and select the HTML source text, open your Web animation HTML file, and paste the text in. Now you have both the animation and the code that runs it.

It's important to follow the instructions that come with applets. Most state that all the files that come with the applets must be in the same directory as your HTML file. Also, Java is very picky about uppercase (capital) and lowercase (small) letters, so, if you need to modify an applet with some of your own graphics, make sure you type your file names accurately.

Once you've copied all your files into the same directory as your HTML file, it's time to modify that HTML file so the browser will call your applet. Here's an example of that sample source code pasted into an HTML file.

```html
<html>

<head>

<title>My Animation Web Site</title>

</head>

<body bgcolor="#FFFFFF">

<div align="center">

    <h1>

    <b><font color="#0000CC">My
    Animation Web Site</font></b>

    </h1>

<applet archive= "ChompText.zip"
code="ChompText.class"

    width=250 height=55>

<param name="text" value="Java
Boutique">

<param name="textcolor"
value="0000FF">

<param name="bgcolor"
value="FFFFFF">

</applet>

</div>

</body>

</html>
```

When you view the HTML file in a browser, you'll see the little yellow Pacman guy eating the text Java Boutique. But you want the little guy to chow down on your text. Go back to your HTML code and find the parameter for changing the text:

```
<param name="text" value="Java
Boutique">
```

and change it to:

```
<param name="text" value="Great
Band Candy On Sale and Going Fast">
```

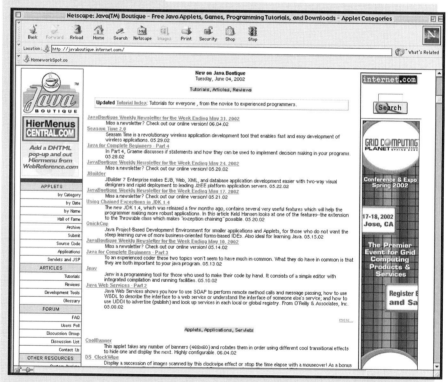

Java Boutique

Java Boutique is one of the one-stop Web sites for useful Java applets. These applets make adding special effects to your site an easy task.

But when you see the animation, you see only half the sentence. You need to make the pixel width of the animation greater. Go back to your code and change the following line from this

```
width=250 height=55>
```

to this (more than doubling the width of your banner)

```
width=525 height=55>
```

You can also go in and fool around with the text color and background color by altering these lines:

```
<param name="textcolor"
value="0000FF">

<param name="bgcolor"
value="FFFFFF">
```

Hex Colors Help:
Macs and PCs often treat colors differently, but hex colors are the same across both computer platforms. Color away, and know that everyone will have a clue to the hue.

The browser reads colors not by name but by a six-digit combination of numbers and letters called hex values. FFFFFF equals white. 0000FF equals a medium blue. There are books and Web pages out there that will show you all the hex numbers for all the colors available in the Web palette. One site that lists 216 hex colors is

http://www.habanero.com/hex

That's all there is to locating and downloading a Java applet to your Web site and then running it. Half the fun of working with these little programs is sampling them and getting ideas that are sure to add some special effects and surprises to your Web page.

Chapter 6

JavaScript

Although they share the same name, Java applets and JavaScript don't have much in common—except that they both can help you to create some pretty cool animation effects and interactive surprises for your Web page.

JavaScript has become one of the most popular Web programming languages on the Internet. It is easier to use than Java applets. If you've ever visited a Web site and discovered that a button or text changes when your mouse cursor rolls over it, or if you've clicked on an animation and made it stop and start, then you've seen some examples of what JavaScript can do.

JavaScript can be written as part of the HTML document and is "read" by the browser along with the HTML. Unlike Java applets, JavaScript actually shows the code. You can easily cut and paste the code from one HTML file to another in order to add effects to your page.

JavaScript was developed by Netscape to improve HTML. Internet Explorer soon made it so its browser could also accept JavaScript code, although some scripts that work with Netscape might not work in Internet Explorer and vice versa. One of the drawbacks of using JavaScript is that it might not be compatible with all browsers. If you decide your Web page needs some JavaScript effects, it's best to test them on the browsers you think your visitors will be using to make sure they work properly.

You don't need to have years of programming experience to use JavaScript to create interactive elements or animations on your Web site. When you work with a Java applet, you download a CLASS file and never see the code. But with JavaScript, you copy the code directly into your HTML and then modify it for use with your graphics or text preferences. You can learn JavaScript in much the same way you learn HTML: by viewing the code and experimenting with all the different options available.

Sharing:
There are lots of sites out there that share JavaScript code and let you cut and paste it to your page for free. As always, give credit where credit is due.

One of JavaScript's most popular functions is making pages more interactive. For example, your visitor rolls the cursor over some text, and it changes color or a picture appears. If you want some information about your visitors, you can offer a short form for them to fill out. Because JavaScript has both date and time features, you can create a calendar or clock or even timestamp a downloaded document.

Now, we'll show you how JavaScript works. One of its most popular effects is making an image on your Web page change when you roll the cursor over it. If you use animated GIFs, you can even make a still image become animated when the cursor rolls over it. We'll show you how to do this and make the GIF animation a link to another Web page by using the "My Favorite Movies" GIF animation we built earlier.

We're going to start with this bit of HTML code that we used in chapter 3.

```
<html>
<head>
<title>My Animation Web
Site</title>
</head>
  <body bgcolor="#FFFFFF">
    <div align="center">
      <img src="movieanim.gif"
      width="215" height="50">
    </div>
  </body>
</html>
```

Let's delete the <img src> line of code because we're going to replace the GIF animation "My Favorite Movies" with a still image that will animate only when the cursor moves over it. Now the code looks like this:

```
<html>
<head>
<title>My Animation Web Site</title>
</head>
      <body bgcolor="#FFFFFF">
          <div align="center">

          </div>
      </body>
</html>
```

Then we'll save this file as my_javascript.htm.

Below is a list of all the files we will use to make the "My Favorite Movies" marquee become animated only when the user rolls the cursor over it.

- my_javascript.htm *(the file into which we'll type the code)*
- movie01.gif *(the still image of "My Favorite Movies" that will sit on the page)*
- movieanim.gif *(the GIF animation that will play when the user rolls the cursor over the still image movie01.GIF)*
- my_favoritemovies.htm *(the Web page you want users to go to when they click on the animated GIF)*

After opening the my_javascript.htm file, we'll type in the JavaScript code after the <div align="center"> tag, because we still want the image centered at the top of the page. Now, the code looks like this:

```
<html>
<head>
<title>My Animation Web Site</title>
</head>
  <body bgcolor="#FFFFFF">
    <div align="center">
    <A HREF="my_favoritemovies.htm"
    onMouseOver="movie.src='movieani
    m.Gif'"onMouseOut="movie.src='mo
    vie01.gif'" >
    <IMG NAME="movie"
    SRC="movie01.gif" WIDTH=215
    HEIGHT=50 BORDER=0></A>
    </div>
  </body>
</html>
```

What does all that mean? Let's go over it line by line.

- <A HREF="my_favoritemovies.htm" *(This is where we put the name of the page we want users to go to when they click on the animation.)*
- onMouseOver="movie.src='movieanim.Gif'" *(onMouseOver means that when the cursor moves over the image we want the movieanim.GIF to play.)*
- onMouseOut="movie.src='movie01.gif'" > *(When the cursor is no longer over the image, we want the animation to stop and the still image "movie01.gif" to be there.)*
- <IMG NAME="movie" SRC="movie01.gif" *(This line makes sure that the still image "movie01.gif" is the one that appears when users first access the page. If we put movieanim.gif there instead, then the animation would play when users access the page.)*
- WIDTH=215 HEIGHT=50 BORDER=0> </A> *(This refers to the width and height of the image. If you decide to copy this code from a free source on the Web, you'll need to change this to fit the image size on your page. BORDER=0 means there's no border around your image. If you change this to, say, BORDER=2, you'll have a 2-pixel-wide border around your image.)*

There are a few things to watch out for. Some HTML files end in .htm and some in .html. Make sure you type your file name accurately.

Also, JavaScript is case sensitive. This means you have to watch whether to use CAPITAL

LETTERS (like those) or small letters (like these) in your file names. Make sure you type in the file names correctly, or the browser won't recognize them. We kept all the letters in our file names lowercase to avoid confusion.

If you use transparent GIFs for your images, the onMouseOver and onMouseOut images will both be visible at the same time.

This example of JavaScript code was very simple. Other special effects and functions are much more complex. The good thing is that you don't have to type lots of lines of code; you can copy code from Web sites that offer it for free. Please make sure that the authors are offering it for free (stealing code is wrong), and always give the author credit. Usually, they'll include this credit as part of the code you copy and paste.

Typing "JavaScripts, free, download" into your search engine will show you many free sites. (Do this with an adult so you don't end up at an inappropriate site.) One site that offers many free JavaScripts and JavaScript writing tools is

http://www.a1javascripts.com

The Web site we mentioned in chapter 3, http://www.lissaexplains.com/intro.shtml, has some very nice effects available, such as making snow fall on your Web page.

Working with JavaScript lets you add exciting animation and interactive elements to your Web site. By experimenting, you can discover all sorts of new ideas that will turn your Web page into a fun and original place for your friends and family to visit.

Chapter 7

Flash and QuickTime

GIFs, Java, and JavaScript aren't the only formats you can use to create animations on the Web. Some formats need special software "players" that are plugged into your browser. We'll talk about two of the most popular ones in this chapter, Flash and QuickTime.

▶ Flash

It's almost impossible to explore the Internet these days and not come across a Flash-animated Web site. You can use this program to create animations, games, slide shows, or entire Web sites. Flash can handle just about anything you can think of to put on the Web or a CD-ROM.

The file sizes for Flash applications are very small—ideal for viewing over the Internet. However, you have to wait for the entire application to load before you get to see or do anything. How long that takes depends on your modem speed and the size of the Flash file.

You need to buy the Flash program software in order to create Flash animations and applications. It's more expensive than your average GIF animation-building program. If you want to learn to create more complex animations, user-controlled Web sites, and games, it might be worth the price.

Macromedia, the company that makes Flash, includes lessons with the program to help you learn how to use it. You can master the basics in a fairly short time.

Your animations can be drawn in Flash itself using its art tools. You can also bring in drawings you created with another paint program. You can use photos and digital video and add sound to the animation as well.

To view Flash applications over the Internet, you need a Flash Player (also referred to as a "plug-in") installed in your browser. The Player is free to download from Macromedia's Web site (http://www.macromedia.com). If you want to look at some Flash effects, go to

http://www.macromedia.com/showcase/

Another way to see examples of Flash is to type "Flash animation" into any kid-oriented search engine. You'll find lots of Flash games and other effects.

Since you can't be sure all the visitors to your site have the player installed, you should include a link to the Macromedia site from your page so they can get it. It's a small file and doesn't take long to download and install. Even so, some of your visitors might be put off by this extra step needed to view your content. On the bright side, many of the later Web browsers have recognized the popularity of this format. They include Flash Players in their browser's package.

Flash to Fame:
Because of the large number of professional-looking effects that can be built with Flash, programmers who have mastered the format are in demand in the computer graphics business.

▶ QuickTime

Created by Apple Computer, QuickTime is one of the most popular presentation formats. It is used to view animations as well as digital video and audio over the Internet.

For some QuickTime examples, go to:

http://www.apple.com/quicktime/

By typing "QuickTime" into Yahoo's search box, you'll find a lot of helpful sites.

QuickTime Streamer:
QuickTime animations take advantage of streaming technology. That means that you can view them as they download onto your page.

You can create QuickTime movies of your animations using a variety of programs. One, called QuickTime Pro, is inexpensive and can be downloaded from Apple's Web site. Another animation trick is to load a series of still pictures showing an action sequence into QuickTime's slideshow. You can vary the "length of time on screen" for each shot to re-create the action. The animation file can be larger than usual because QuickTime can stream your file to a visitor's computer without the long wait for a complete download. That means you can add music and sound effects to your animation without worrying about a big fat file. If you're using an older browser, you'll need to download a QuickTime Player plug-in. You can download it for free from Apple's site. Most of the newer browsers come with it. Here's a guide to help you keep track of which browser version works with which type of animation. For Flash and QuickTime, check your browser.

Internet Addresses   Communication Facts   How Can I Be Safe?

Browsers	Technology		
	GIF89a	Java Applets	JavaScript
Internet Explorer v3 through v6	X	X	X
Netscape/Navigator v2 through v6.1	X	X	X
Mozilla	X	X	X
AOL Browser 5			X
Opera 4.02 through 5.11	X	X	somewhat

▶ Conclusion

We've seen only the tip of the iceberg when it comes to animation on the Web. With ever-changing technology, it's hard to keep up with all the changes and updates. We're enjoying faster connection speeds, more efficient file compression formats, streaming technology, compatible browsers, and more. The opportunities for creativity and exploration are limitless. We've given you a few tools to get you started, but the limitations described in this book are disappearing fast, so the sky's the limit.

The best part of creating animation for your Web site is experimenting. Try some of the animation programs we've described. Download a few GIFs and JavaScripts. Have fun with the process, because you control virtually everything. But be careful. Creating your first animation is like eating one potato chip: You just want more and more. Once you add that first simple GIF, you see the possibilities for an all-singing, all-dancing Web site. Take pity on your poor visitor! One good idea is to build a library of animations and use only a couple at a time on your site. Change them every couple of weeks or so.

Keep your site fresh and full of surprises. Pretty soon, you'll have other sites asking if they can link to yours. That's when you know your Web site is a rousing success. Animation is one of the tools that make Web sites fun to visit and even more fun to create.

Glossary

applet—Self-contained application written in Java code that can be called up by your HTML code to perform a special function or effect.

application—Complete software program created to do a particular job, such as give you an on-screen sound control panel for your audio files.

authoring tools—Programs that help you build a Web site, animation effects, or other special effects, such as putting frames into sequence to create a GIF animation.

compress—Make a large file smaller using a special program called a codec (compression/decompression). With photos and graphics, pixels are removed. In audio, bits are removed. And in video, frames are disposed of to reduce the size of the file.

cycle—Complete series of animated movements from beginning to end. The cycle can be "looped" to create a continuous animation on screen until halted by a command.

frame—Element in a sequence of elements used to create an animation. For example: boywalking 01, boywalking 02, boywalking 03, and boywalking 04 are four frames that make up the animation showing a boy walking.

interactive—Word describing a site that asks the visitor to do something, such as click on a button, roll a cursor arrow over a space, or fill out a form to make something happen. He or she interacts with your Web site.

marquee—Animation that shows flashing lights or lights changing colors. Usually these lights appear to move around a word or words that you want to focus people's attention on.

paint program—Any software program used to create or manipulate graphics from very simple applications that come with most computer operating systems to sophisticated programs such as Photoshop or Corel Draw.

palette—Any grouping of colors, usually arranged in a particular order.

reassemble—To put back together something that has been taken apart.

rollover—An effect that you can create on your Website, such that when the visitor moves the cursor over a particular element (button, photo, text), something happens. For example: when the cursor goes over Jane's picture, Jane says "Hello."

script—A Java-coded program that may be typed directly into an HTML-coded program to create a special effect. The Java Script code can be seen and changed if needed, unlike the hidden code in a Java applet.

stream—Send a large file, such as a video program or complex animation, from the Web site to your computer in a continuous flow so that you watch the beginning while the middle and end are arriving. Downloading requires you to make room for the entire file before viewing it, often making for a long wait.

tweening—Animation frames that go in between key frames to make the animated motion smooth instead of choppy.

utility—Any program that performs a simple job, such as a compression/decompression utility–or codec–that makes a file smaller and then restores the file to virtually its original size.

Further Reading

Ashdown, David. *HyperStudio Made Very Easy!* New York: Scholastic Professional Books, 2000.

Basch, Reva, and Mary Ellen Bates. *Researching Online for Dummies.* Foster City, Calif.: IDG Books Worldwide, 2000.

Dawson, Dennis, and Mark Kistler. *Mark Kistler's Web Wizards.* New York: Fireside, 2000.

Flynn, Mike. *Inside a Web Site.* Danbury, Conn.: Grolier Educational, 2001.

Hafkemeyer, Christof. *The Internet: Surfin' the Web.* Nuremburg, Germany: Tessloff, 1998.

Lindsay, Bruce, and Dave Lindsay. *Dave's Quick 'n' Easy Web Pages.* Calgary, Canada: Erin Publications.

Moss, Francis, and Ted Pederson. *Make Your Own Web Page: A Guide for Kids.* New York: Price, Stern, Sloan, 1998.

Trumbauer, Lisa. *Cool Sites, Free Stuff for Kids on the Net.* Brookfield, Conn.: Millbrook Press, 1999.

White, Tony. *The Animator's Workbook.* New York: Watson-Guptill Publications, 1986.

Index